MUSIC ON WINGS
PIANO BEGINNER COURSE

STUDENT GUIDE BOOK 2

Teresa Wong

THIS BOOK BELONGS TO:

Copyright © 2016 - 2019 Wong Wing Yin
All rights reserved.
ISBN: 978-988-77083-3-9

Sixth Edition

Author: Teresa Wing-Yin Wong
Publishing Assistant: Cheeky Kea Printworks

INTRODUCTION

ABOUT MUSIC ON WINGS PIANO BEGINNER COURSE

Music on Wings Piano Beginner Course is an all-in-one piano course that provides a comprehensive training in all aspects of music learning: playing, listening, singing, reading, writing, improvising and composing. It is created to benefit both teachers and students so that optimum result is maximized through precision teaching, learning and practice.

STUDENT PRACTICE GUIDE BOOK SERIES

This comprehensive series provides students with step-by-step practice notes to enable independent, at home revision. Each practice session is specifically designed to give both students and parents the confidence that improvement through precise practice will be achieved each and every time. This guide will give every student a solid foundation in piano playing and musical knowledge, bringing even greater enjoyment to piano learning.

STUDENT PRACTICE GUIDE: BOOK II

Book II is the second in this series of four books, each one advancing students to a higher level of music understanding and piano performance. This is a fun and easy-to-use book that enables piano beginners of all ages to embark on a new and exciting musical journey.

There are four sections in this book: repertoire playing (pieces and practice directions); aural training (singing and listening); sight-reading (note reading and rhythm training); and technique training (scales and exercises).

Best results will be achieved by following the step-by-step practice instructions and doing all the home exercises, which in turn will transform lessons into amazingly productive and enjoyable development sessions.

POSTURE

1. Sit up straight from the lower back and all the way through your neck up to top of your head.

2. Make sure that your feet are planted firmly on the floor. If your feet cannot reach the floor, use a foot stool.

3. Keep both feet firmly on the ground or stool at all times, maintaining a strong connection between you, the ground/stool and the piano.

4. Relax. Keep your shoulders down and open your chest to receive beautiful music from the piano!

TECHNIQUE

1. Curl your fingers down, keeping your palms in a round shape (ball shape).

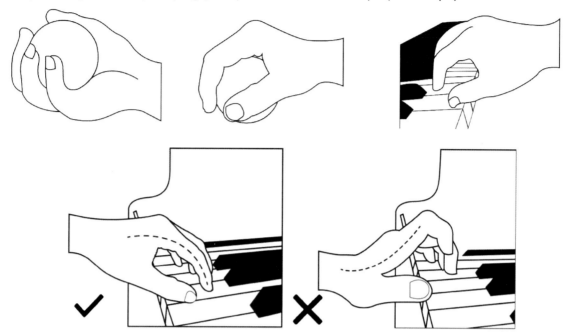

2. Keep some space between your upper arms and your upper torso.

3. Suspending your upper arms in the air will help you engage your whole body in your playing.

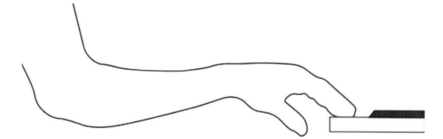

4. Make sure that your forearms remain more or less parallel to the ground.

5. Your wrists should be in a straight line with your forearms at the starting position, and then they remain "bouncy" (supple/flexible) the whole time when you play This allows you to channel the full strength of your body, from your legs, lower and upper torsos, through your arms and down into your fingertips, connecting your whole self with the piano and the music.

INDEX

LESSON 1

25-30 MINUTES

1. WARM-UP EXERCISE (TECHNIQUE EXERCISE, P.69) [5 MINUTES]

Ex.2a
Practice the exercise 3 times (slow version 1 beat=60)
Practice the exercise 2 times (fast version 1 beat=92)

Ex.2b
Practice the exercise 3 times (slow version 1 beat=60)
Practice the exercise 2 times (fast version 1 beat=92)

2. G MAJOR SCALE (1 OCTAVE) (P.74) [5 MINUTES]

a. Sing the scale in solfège

b. RIGHT HAND: Going up and down, G4 - G5 (3 times)

c. LEFT HAND: Going up and down, G3 - G4 (3 times)

3. SONG: YANKEE DOODLE (P.4) [15 MINUTES]

RIGHT HAND

SECTION 1		
PHRASE 1:	G G A B G B A D	G G A B G F# D
PHRASE 2:	G G A B C B A G F# D E F# G G	
SECTION 2		
PHRASE 3:	E F# E D E F# G	E D E D C B C D
PHRASE 4:	E F# E D E F# G	E D G F# A G G

a. Practice phrase 1 (5 times)

b. Practice phrase 2 (5 times)   💡 *Phrase 2's hand position is different from phrase 1's !*

c. Practice section 1: phrases 1 and 2 (5 times)

d. Practice phrase 3 (5 times)

e. Practice phrase 4 (5 times)

f. Practice section 2: phrases 3 and 4 (5 times)

g. *CHALLENGE* : Practice the whole song smoothly 3 times!

4. THEORY TIME [5 MINUTES]
A SCALE HAS 7 DIFFERENT NOTES. THIS IS THE PATTERN FOR A MAJOR SCALE:
(W=WHOLE STEP, H=HALF STEP)

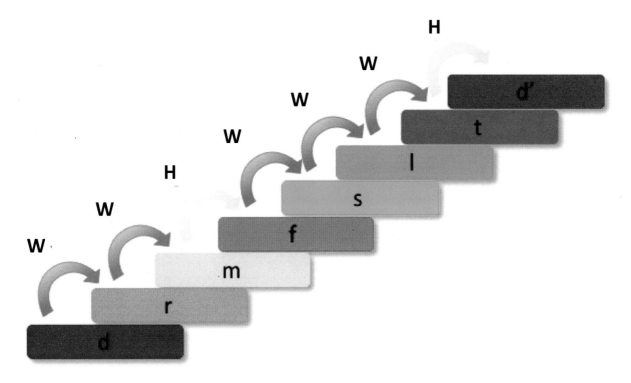

Color the keys that make up a C major scale.

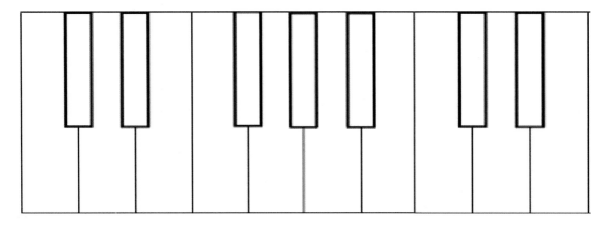

Color the keys that make up a G major scale.

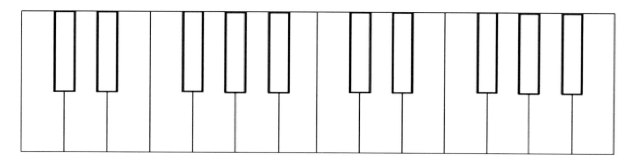

 For advanced students: Color the keys that make up a _____ major scale.

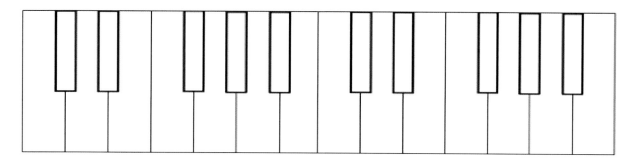

 5. SIGHT-READING (P.76) [5 MINUTES]

Ex. 1 and 2
Check before you play!
1. Are they treble and bass clefs?

2. Look at the key signature

3. Look at the time signature

4. Find the first notes for both hands on the keyboard

5. Place you hands on the starting position

6. Count 2 bars before playing

7. You can start now

YANKEE DOODLE

Arr. Teresa Wong

PRACTICE RECORD

	Day 1	Day 2	Day 3	Day 4	Day 5	Day 6	Day 7
1							
2							
3							
4							
5							

STUDENT'S COMMENTS	TEACHER'S COMMENTS

LESSON 2

20-30 MINUTES

1. **WARM-UP EXERCISE (TECHNIQUE EXERCISE, P.69) [5 MINUTES]**
   Ex. 1b
   Play the exercise 3 times (1 beat=80)

2. **G MAJOR SCALE: SIMILAR MOTION, GOING UP (1 OCTAVE) (P.74) [5 MINUTES]**
   Hands together: LEFT HAND starting on G3 and RIGHT HAND starting on G4 (3 times)

3. **SONG: YANKEE DOODLE (P.4) [15 MINUTES]**

   LEFT HAND

SECTION 1		
PHRASE 1:	B - C - B ---	B - C - B ---
	G - G - G ---	G - G - G ---
PHRASE 2:	B --- C ---	C --- B ---
	G --- G ---	G --- G ---
SECTION 2		
PHRASE 3:	C --- C ---	B --- B ---
	G --- G ---	G --- G ---
PHRASE 4:	C --- C ---	B - C - B ---
	G --- G ---	G - G - G ---

   a. Practice section 1 (5 times)

   b. Practice section 2 (5 times)

   c. Practice sections 1 and 2 (5 times)

   d. Practice hands together phrase by phrase (5 times)

 e. *CHALLENGE*: Play the whole song hands together smoothly 5 times!

4. THEORY TIME: ACCIDENTALS

Sharp (♯): raises a note by one half step
Flat (♭): lowers a note by one half step
Natural (♮): cancels out a sharp or flat

Add a sharp (♯) before each note and write down the letter name of each note in the box provided.

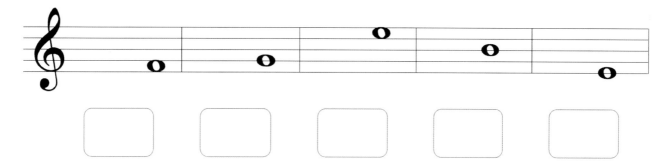

Add a flat (♭) before each note and write down the letter name of each note in the box provided.

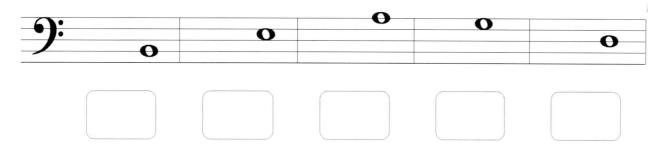

Add a natural (♮) before each note and write down the letter name of each note in the box provided.

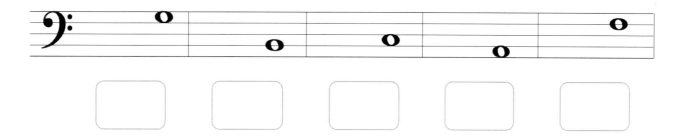

CIRCLE THE CORRECT LETTER NAMES.

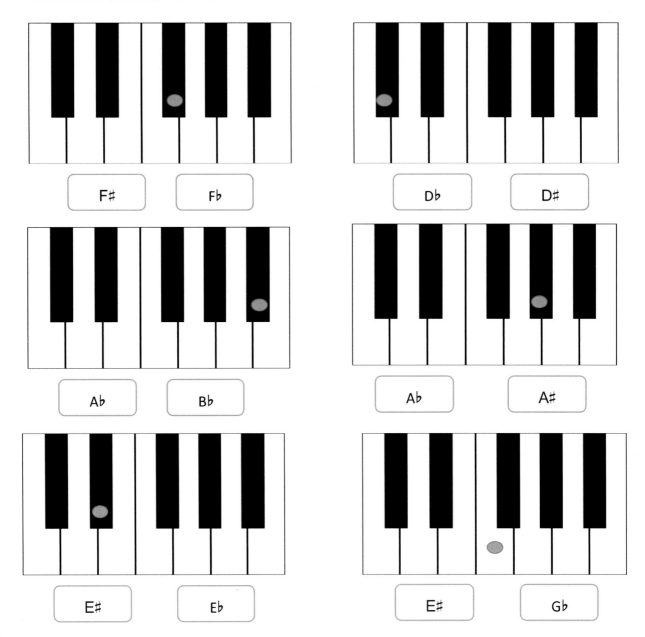

F#	Fb		Db	D#

Ab	Bb		Ab	A#

E#	Eb		E#	Gb

5. SIGHT-READING (P.76) [5 MINUTES]

Ex. 3 and 4

Check before you play!

1. Are they treble and bass clefs?

2. Look at the key signature

3. Look at the time signature

4. Find the first notes for both hands on the keyboard

5. Place your hands on the starting position

6. Count 2 bars before playing

7. You can start now

PRACTICE RECORD

	Day 1	Day 2	Day 3	Day 4	Day 5	Day 6	Day 7
1							
2							
3							
4							
5							

STUDENT'S COMMENTS	TEACHER'S COMMENTS

LESSON 3

20-30 MINUTES

1. **WARM-UP EXERCISE (TECHNIQUE EXERCISE, P.69 AND 70) [5 MINUTES]**
   Ex.2b (P.69)
   Practice the exercise 3 times

   Ex.4a (P.70)
   Practice the exercise 3 times

2. **G MAJOR SCALE SIMILAR MOTION: GOING DOWN (1 OCTAVE) (P.74) [5 MINUTES]**
   Hands together: LEFT HAND starting on G4 and RIGHT HAND starting on G5 (3 times)

3. **SONG: G MAJOR WALTZ (P.12) [10 MINUTES]**

   RIGHT HAND
   a. Practice bars 1-4 (5 times)
   b. Practice bars 5-8 (5 times)
   c. Practice bars 9-12 (5 times)
   d. Practice bars 13-17 (5 times)
   e. Practice bars 1-8 (3 times)
   f. Practice bars 9-17 (3 times)
   g. *CHALLENGE* : Practice the whole song smoothly 3 times!

   LEFT HAND
   h. Practice this four-bar chord pattern (5 times)

   i. Practice this four-bar chord pattern (5 times)

HANDS TOGETHER
a. Practice bars 1-4 (5 times)
b. Practice bars 5-8 (5 times)
c. Practice bars 9-12 (5 times)
d. Practice bars 13-17 (5 times)
e. Practice bars 1-8 (3 times)
f. Practice bars 9-17 (3 times)
g. *CHALLENGE* : Practice the whole song smoothly 3 times!

4. THEORY TIME

Use half notes (𝅗𝅥) to write a G major scale (going down) on the staff, remember to add accidentals if necessary.

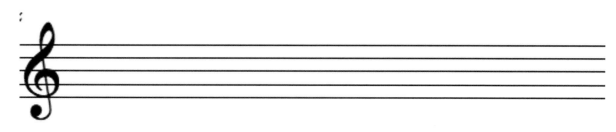

Use quarter notes (𝅘𝅥) to write a G major scale (going up) on the staff, remember to add accidentals if necessary.

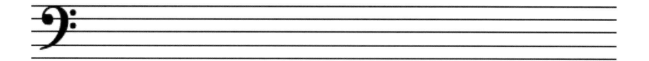

5. SIGHT-READING (P.77) [5 MINUTES]
Ex. 5 and 6
Check before you play!
1. Are they treble and bass clefs?
2. Look at the key signature
3. Look at the time signature
4. Find the first notes for both hands on the keyboard
5. Place your hands on the starting position
6. Count 2 bars before playing
7. You can start now

G MAJOR WALTZ

Teresa Wong

PRACTICE RECORD

	Day 1	Day 2	Day 3	Day 4	Day 5	Day 6	Day 7
1							
2							
3							
4							
5							

STUDENT'S COMMENTS	TEACHER'S COMMENTS

LESSON 4

25-30 MINUTES

 1. **WARM-UP EXERCISE (TECHNIQUE EXERCISE, P.72 AND 73) [5 MINUTES]**
Exercise in 5ths (a) (P.72)
Practice the exercise 3 times (1 beat=60)

Two-note Variation (P.73)
Practice the exercise 3 times

2. **G MAJOR SCALE SIMILAR MOTION: GOING UP AND DOWN (1 OCTAVE) (P.74) [5 MINUTES]**
Hands together: LEFT HAND starting on G3 and RIGHT HAND starting on G4 (3 times)

 3. **SONG: OH SUZANNA (P.16) [15 MINUTES]**

RIGHT HAND
a.   Practice phrase 1, bars 1-4 (5 times)
b.   Practice phrase 2, bars 5-8 (5 times)
c.   Practice phrase 3, bars 9-12 (5 times)
d.   Practice phrase 4, bars 13-16 (5 times)
e.   Practice phrases 1-2 (3 times)
f.   Practice phrases 3-4 (3 times)
g.   *CHALLENGE* : Play the whole song smoothly 3 times!

4. THEORY TIME: TIME SIGNATURES
Complete the time signatures below.

5. SIGHT-READING (P.77) [5 MINUTES]
Ex. 7 and 8

Check before you play!
1. Are they treble and bass clefs?
2. Look at the key signature
3. Look at the time signature
4. Find the first notes for both hands on the keyboard
5. Place your hands on the starting position
6. Count 2 bars before playing
7. You can start now

OH SUZANNA

Arr. Teresa Wong

PRACTICE RECORD

	Day 1	Day 2	Day 3	Day 4	Day 5	Day 6	Day 7
1							
2							
3							
4							
5							

STUDENT'S COMMENTS	TEACHER'S COMMENTS

LESSON 5

25-30 MINUTES

1. **WARM-UP EXERCISE (TECHNIQUE EXERCISE, P.72) [5 MINUTES]**
   Broken Chord
   Practice the exercise 3 times (1 beat=60)

   One-note Variation (a)
   Practice the exercise 2 times

2. **G MAJOR ARPEGGIOS: GOING UP AND DOWN (1 OCTAVE) (P.75) [5 MINUTES]**
   a. RIGHT HAND: Starting on G4 (5 times)
   b. LEFT HAND: Starting on G3 (5 times)

3. **SONG: OH SUZANNA (P.16) [15 MINUTES]**
   LEFT HAND
   1. Practice bars 1-4 (5 times)
   2. Practice bars 5-8 (5 times)
   3. Practice bars 9-12 (5 times)
   4. Practice bars 13-16 (5 times)
   5. Practice bars 1-8 (3 times)
   6. Practice bars 9-16 (3 times)
    7. *CHALLENGE* : Play the whole song smoothly 3 times!

   HANDS TOGETHER
   8. Practice phrase 1 (5 times)
   9. Practice phrase 2 (5 times)
   10. Practice phrase 3 (5 times)
   11. Practice phrase 4 (5 times)
   12. Practice phrases 1-2 (3 times)
   13. Practice phrases 3-4 (3 times)
    14. *CHALLENGE* : Play the whole song smoothly 2 times!

4. THEORY TIME: BAR LINES
Add the missing bar lines.

5. SIGHT-READING (P.78) [5 MINUTES]
EX. 9 and 10

Check before you play!

1. Are they treble and bass clefs?

2. Look at the key signature

3. Look at the time signature

4. Find the first notes for both hands on the keyboard

5. Place your hands on the starting position

6. Count 2 bars before playing

7. You can start now

PRACTICE RECORD

	Day 1	Day 2	Day 3	Day 4	Day 5	Day 6	Day 7
1							
2							
3							
4							
5							

STUDENT'S COMMENTS	TEACHER'S COMMENTS

LESSON 6

25-30 MINUTES

1. **WARM-UP EXERCISE (TECHNIQUE EXERCISE, P.72 AND 69) [5 MINUTES]**
   Exercise in 5ths (a) (P.72)
   Practice the exercise 3 times (1 beat=92)

   EX.3A Three Notes (P.69)
   Practice the exercise 3 times

2. **G MAJOR SCALES: GOING UP AND DOWN (2 OCTAVES) (P.74) [5 MINUTES]**
   RIGHT HAND: Starting on G4: G4-G6 (5 times)

3. **SONG: LONG LONG AGO (P.23-24) [15 MINUTES]**
   RIGHT HAND
   a. Practice phrase 1 (5 times)
   b. Practice phrase 2 (5 times)
   c. Practice phrase 3 (5 times)
   d. Practice phrase 4 (5 times)
   e. Practice phrases 1-2 (3 times)
   f. Practice phrases 3-4 (3 times)

   g. CHALLENGE: Play the whole song smoothly 2 times!

4. THEORY TIME   [10 MINUTES]
Add one note in each box provided.

5. SIGHT-READING (P.78) [5 MINUTES]
Ex. 11 and 12
Check before you play!
1. Are they treble and bass clefs?

2. Look at the key signature

3. Look at the time signature

4. Find the first notes for both hands on the keyboard

5. Place your hands on the starting position

6. Count 2 bars before playing

7. You can start now

LONG LONG AGO

Thomas Haynes Bayly
Arr. Teresa Wong

(Level 1 – Block Chord Pattern)

LONG LONG AGO

(Level 2 – Alberti Bass Pattern)

PRACTICE RECORD

	Day 1	Day 2	Day 3	Day 4	Day 5	Day 6	Day 7
1							
2							
3							
4							
5							

STUDENT'S COMMENTS	TEACHER'S COMMENTS

LESSON 7

25-30 MINUTES

 1. WARM-UP EXERCISE (TECHNIQUE EXERCISE, P.72) [5 MINUTES]
Broken Chord
Practice the exercise 3 times (1 beat=92)

2. G MAJOR SCALE (2 OCTAVES) (P.74) [5 MINUTES]
LEFT HAND: Starting on G2 going up to G4 and going down to G2 (5 times)

 3. SONG: LONG LONG AGO (P.23-24) [15 MINUTES]
LEFT HAND
Level 1: Block-Chord Pattern
a. Practice bars 1-4 (5 times)
b. Practice bars 5-8 (5 times)
c. Practice bars 9-12 (5 times)
d. Practice bars 13-16 (5 times)

HANDS TOGETHER
e. Practice phrase 1 (5 times)
f. Practice phrase 2 (5 times)
g. Practice phrase 3 (5 times)
h. Practice phrase 4 (5 times)
i. Practice phrase 1-2 (3 times)
j. Practice phrases 3-4 (3 times)
 k. *CHALLENGE*: Play the whole song smoothly 2 times!

ADVANCED STUDENTS CAN TRY:
LEVEL 2: ALBERTI BASS PATTERN
Practice bars 1-4 (5 times)
Practice bars 5-8 (5 times)

4. THEORY TIME: HARMONIC INTERVALS

Write down the degree of each interval (2nd, 3rd, 4th, 5th, 6th, 7th, 8^{ve}) for each pair of notes in the box provided.

5. SIGHT-READING (P.79) [5 MINUTES]

EX. 13 and 14

Check before you play!

1. Are they treble and bass clefs?

2. Look at the key signature

3. Look at the time signature

4. Find the first notes for both hands on the keyboard

5. Place your hands on the starting position

6. Count 2 bars before playing

7. You can start now

PRACTICE RECORD

	Day 1	Day 2	Day 3	Day 4	Day 5	Day 6	Day 7
1							
2							
3							
4							
5							

STUDENT'S COMMENTS	TEACHER'S COMMENTS

LESSON 8

25-30 MINUTES

1. **WARM-UP EXERCISE (TECHNIQUE EXERCISE, P.70) [5 MINUTES]**
   EX.4a
   Practice the exercise 3 times

2. **F MAJOR SCALE (1 OCTAVE) (P.74) [5 MINUTES]**
   a. Sing the scale in solfège
   b. RIGHT HAND: Going up from F4 to F5 and going down from F5 to F4 (3 times)
   c. LEFT HAND: Going up from F3 to F4 and going down from F4 to F3 (3 times)

3. **SONG: STARLIGHT WALTZ: SECTION 1 (P.31) [15 MINUTES]**
   RIGHT HAND
   a. Practice RIGHT HAND bars 1-7 (5 times)
   b. Practice RIGHT HAND bars 8-16 (5 times)

   LEFT HAND
   c. Fill in the missing notes of LEFT HAND pattern from bars 1 – 16

   d. Practice the above pattern (5 times)

   HANDS TOGETHER
   e. Practice bars 1-3 (5 times)
   f. Practice bars 4-7 (5 times)
   g. Practice bars 8-11 (5 times)
   h. Practice bars 12-16 (5 times)
   i. Feel the pulse (ONE-TWO-THREE) and practice bars 1-16 (3 times)

4. THEORY TIME : MELODIC INTERVALS

Write down the degree of each interval (2nd, 3rd, 4th, 5th, 6th, 7th, 8^{ve}) for each pair of notes in the box provided.

5. SIGHT-READING (P.79) [5 MINUTES]

EX. 15 and 16

Check before you play!

1. Are they treble and bass clefs?

2. Look at the key signature

3. Look at the time signature

4. Find the first notes for both hands on the keyboard

5. Place your hands on the starting position

6. Count 2 bars before playing

7. You can start now

STARLIGHT WALTZ

C. S. Brainard
Arr. Teresa Wong

STARLIGHT WALTZ

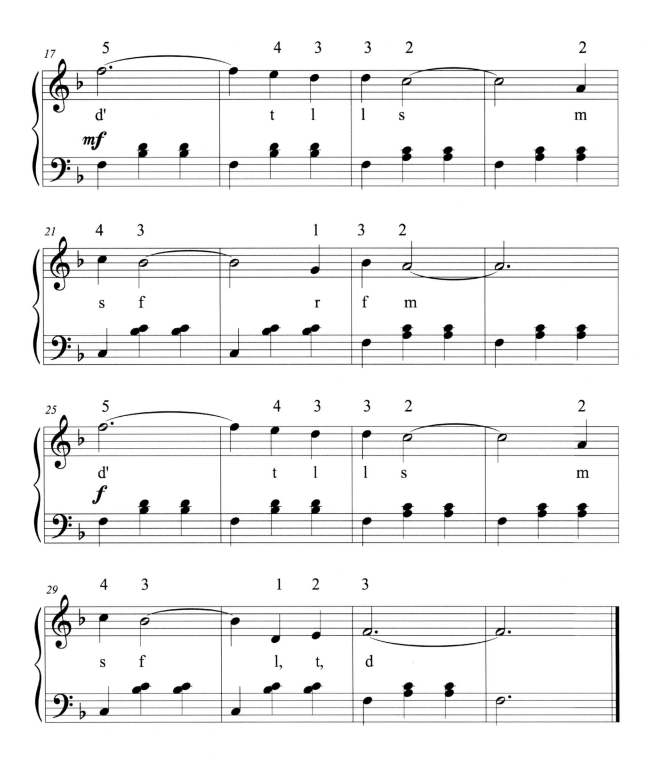

PRACTICE RECORD

	Day 1	Day 2	Day 3	Day 4	Day 5	Day 6	Day 7
1							
2							
3							
4							
5							

STUDENT'S COMMENTS	TEACHER'S COMMENTS

LESSON 9

25-30 MINUTES

1. WARM-UP EXERCISE (TECHNIQUE EXERCISE, P.70) [5 MINUTES]
EX.4B
Practice the exercise 3 times

2. F MAJOR SCALE SIMILAR MOTION GOING UP AND DOWN (1 OCTAVE) (P.74) [5 MINUTES]
RIGHT HAND: Going up from F4 to F5 and going down from F5 to F4 (3 times)
LEFT HAND: Going up from F3 to F4 and going down from F4 to F3 (3 times)
Hands together: LEFT HAND starting on F3 and RIGHT HAND starting on F4 (3 times)

3. SONG: STARLIGHT WALTZ: SECTION 2 (P.32) [15 MINUTES]
RIGHT HAND
a. Practice RIGHT HAND bars 17-24 (5 times)
b. Practice RIGHT HAND bars 25-32 (5 times)
LEFT HAND
c. Fill in the missing notes of LEFT HAND pattern from bars 17-32

d. Practice the above pattern (5 times)

HANDS TOGETHER
a. Practice bars 17-20 (5 times)
b. Practice bars 21-24 (5 times)
c. Practice bars 25-28 (5 times)
d. Practice bars 29-32 (5 times)
e. Feel the pulse (ONE-TWO-THREE) and practice bars 17-32 (3 times)
f. *CHALLENGE*: Play the whole song smoothly 3 times!

4. THEORY TIME: DOTTED NOTES AND TIES

A dot after a note makes it longer by adding half of its value.

	Note	Equal to	
Dotted half note	𝅗𝅥.	𝅗𝅥 + ♩	♩ + ♩ + ♩
Dotted quarter note	♩.	♩ + ♪	♪ + ♪ + ♪
Dotted eighth note	♪.	♪ + ♬	♬ + ♬ + ♬

Fill in the missing notes.

♩ + ☐ = ♩.   𝅗𝅥 + ♩ = ☐

𝅗𝅥 + ☐ = 𝅗𝅥.   ♪ + ♩ = ☐

♪ + ☐ = ♪.   ☐ + ♪ = ♩.

♩ + ♪ = ☐   ☐ + ♬ = ♪.

A tie connects 2 or more notes of the same pitch. The first note is played and held for the length of the whole duration of all the tied notes.

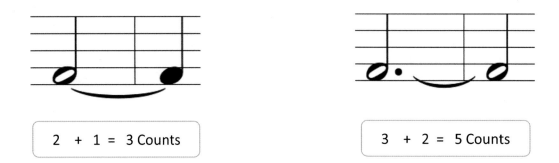

2 + 1 = 3 Counts

3 + 2 = 5 Counts

Count the beats in each star, draw a line to match the correct numbers of the beats in total.

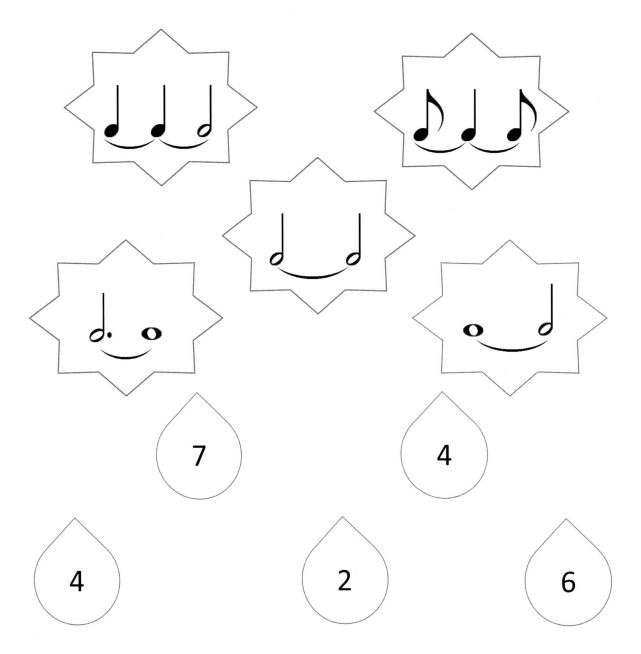

5. SIGHT-READING (P.80) [5 MINUTES]
EX. 17 and 18

Check before you play!

1. Are they treble and bass clefs?

2. Look at the key signature

3. Look at the time signature

4. Find the first notes for both hands on the keyboard

5. Place your hands on the starting position

6. Count 2 bars before playing

7. You can start now

PRACTICE RECORD

	Day 1	Day 2	Day 3	Day 4	Day 5	Day 6	Day 7
1							
2							
3							
4							
5							

STUDENT'S COMMENTS	TEACHER'S COMMENTS

LESSON 10

25-30 MINUTES

1. WARM-UP EXERCISE (TECHNIQUE EXERCISE, P.69 AND 72) [5 MINUTES]

EX. 1b (P.69)
Practice the exercise 3 times (1 beat=80)

Exercise in 5ths (b) (P.72)
Practice the exercise 3 times (1 beat=60)

Exercise in 5ths (c)) (P.72)
Practice the exercise 3 times (1 beat=60)

One-note Variation (b) (P.72)
Practice the exercise 2 times

STACCATO TECHNIQUE
Light touch
Flexible/ supple wrist
Focused fingertips

2. F MAJOR ARPEGGIOS (1 OCTAVE) (P.75) [5 MINUTES]

RIGHT HAND: Starting on F4 going up and down (5 times)
LEFT HAND: Starting on F3 going up and down (5 times)

3. SONG: AUTUMN (FROM "THE FOUR SEASONS"): PART 1 (P.42) [15 MINUTES]

RIGHT HAND
a. Clap this rhythm  (5 times)
b. Practice bars 1-4 (5 times)
c. Practice bars 5-8 (5 times)

LEFT HAND
d. Practice bars 1-4 (5 times)
e. Practice bars 5-8 (5 times)

HANDS TOGETHER
f. Practice bars 1-2 (5 times)
g. Practice bars 3-4 (5 times)
h. Practice bars 1-4 (5 times)
i. Practice bars 5-6 (5 times)
j. Practice bar 7-8 (5 times)
k. Practice bar 5-8 (5 times)
l. Practice bars 1-16 (3 times)

4. THEORY TIME- KEY SIGNATURES

Use whole notes (𝗢) to write an **F major** scale (going up) on the staff below, and remember to add key signature if necessary.

Use half notes (♩) to write a **C major scale** (going up) on the staff below, and remember to add key signature if necessary.

Use quarter notes (♩) to write a **G major** scale (going up) on the staff below, and remember to add key signature if necessary.

Use whole notes (𝗢) to write an **F major** scale (going up) on the staff below, and remember to add key signature if necessary.

Use half notes (♩) to write a **C major** scale (going up) on the staff below, and remember to add key signature if necessary.

Use quarter notes (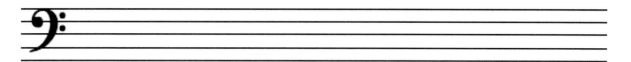) to write a **G major** scale (going up) on the staff below, and remember to add key signature if necessary.

5. SIGHT READING (P.80) [5 MINUTES]
EX. 19 and 20
Check before you play!

a. Are they treble and bass clef?

b. Look at the key signature

c. Look at the time signature

d. Find the first notes for both hands on the keyboard

e. Place your hands on the starting position

f. Count 2 bars before playing

g. You can start now

AUTUMN: PART 1

Vivaldi
Arr. Teresa Wong

AUTUMN: PART 2

PRACTICE RECORD

	Day 1	Day 2	Day 3	Day 4	Day 5	Day 6	Day 7
1							
2							
3							
4							
5							

STUDENT'S COMMENTS	TEACHER'S COMMENTS

LESSON 11

22-30 MINUTES

1. **WARM-UP EXERCISE (TECHNIQUE EXERCISE, P.69 AND 72) [5 MINUTES]**
   EX. 1b (P.69)
   Practice the exercise 3 times (1 beat=80)

   Exercise in 5ths (b) (P.72)
   Practice the exercise 3 times (1 beat=92)

   Exercise in 5ths (c) (P.72)
   Practice the exercise 3 times (1 beat=92)

   One-note Variation (b) (P.72)
   Practice the exercise 2 times

2. **F MAJOR SCALE: GOING UP AND DOWN (2 OCTAVES) (P.75) [5 MINUTES]**
   RIGHT HAND: Starting on F4 (- F6) (5 times)

3. **SONG: AUTUMN (FROM "THE FOUR SEASONS"): PART 2 (P.43) [10 MINUTES]**
   RIGHT HAND
   a. Practice bars 17-18 (5 times)
   b. Practice bars 17-24 (5 times)
   LEFT HAND
   c. Practice bars 17-18 (5 times)
   d. Practice bars 17-24 (5 times)
   HANDS TOGETHER
   e. Practice bars 17-18 (5 times)
   f. Practice bars 17-24 (5 times)

   g. *CHALLENGE*: Play the whole song smoothly 3 times!

4. **THEORY TIME: PHRASES AND STRUCTURE [10 MINUTES]**
   There are four phrases that make up this whole song, so the form of the song is A-A-B-A. Now go write down these letters in the empty boxes at the start of each section in the score.

   PHRASE STRUCTURE
   A = bars 1-8
   A = bars 9-16
   B = bars 17-24
   A = bars 25-32

5. SIGHT-READING (P.81) [5 MINUTES]

EX. 21 and 22

Check before you play!

1. Are they treble and bass clefs?

2. Look at the key signature

3. Look at the time signature

4. Find the first notes for both hands on the keyboard

5. Place your hands on the starting position

6. Count 2 bars before playing

7. You can start now

PRACTICE RECORD

	Day 1	Day 2	Day 3	Day 4	Day 5	Day 6	Day 7
1							
2							
3							
4							
5							

STUDENT'S COMMENTS	TEACHER'S COMMENTS

LESSON 12

25-30 MINUTES

1. **WARM-UP EXERCISE (TECHNIQUE EXERCISE, P.71) [5 MINUTES]**
   EX. 5a Five-note Variation
   Practice the exercise 3 times

2. **F MAJOR SCALE: GOING UP AND DOWN (2 OCTAVES) (P.74) [5 MINUTES]**
   LEFT HAND: Starting on F3 (-F5) (5 times)

3. **SONG: HAPPY BIRTHDAY SONG (P.51) [15 MINUTES]**
   RIGHT HAND
   a.   Sing the melody in solfège
   b.   Practice phrase 1 (5 times)
   c.   Practice phrase 2 (5 times)
   d.   Practice phrase 3 (5 times)
   e.   Practice phrase 4 (5 times)
   f.   Practice phrases 1 and 2 (3 times)
   g.   Practice phrases 3 and 4 (3 times)

   h.   *CHALLENGE:* Play the whole song smoothly 3 times!

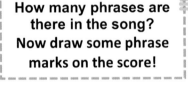

How many phrases are there in the song? Now draw some phrase marks on the score!

   LEFT HAND
   i.   Practice the pattern (5 times)

   HANDS TOGETHER
   j.   Practice each phrase (5 times)

   k.   *CHALLENGE:* Play the whole song smoothly 3 times!

4. IMPROVISATION/ KEYBOARD SKILLS [10 MINUTES]

a. Fill in the missing notes of F and C chords.

b. Try the sequence below (in 4 beats)

| F - - - | C - - - | F - - - | C - F - |

c. How do you make a better melody or more interesting sound? Try making a nice   melody on the right hand with different rhythmic patterns or simple block chords on the left hand!

5. SIGHT READING (P.81) [5 MINUTES]

EX. 23 and 24

Check before you play!

1.   Are they treble and bass clefs?

2.   Look at the key signature

3.   Look at the time signature

4.   Find the first notes for both hands on the keyboard

5.   Place your hands on the starting position

6.   Count 2 bars before playing

7.   You can start now

6. THEORY TIME: TRIADS (CHORDS)
A triad has 3 different notes:
1st degree **+** the 3rd degree above **+** the 5th degree above

Write the name of each chord in the box, and the letters that go with it in the circles.

Chords

C

G

E

C

Chords

HAPPY BIRTHDAY SONG

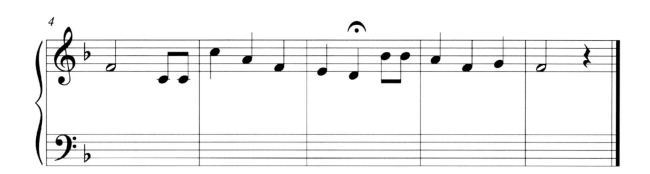

PRACTICE RECORD

	Day 1	Day 2	Day 3	Day 4	Day 5	Day 6	Day 7
1							
2							
3							
4							
5							

STUDENT'S COMMENTS	TEACHER'S COMMENTS

LESSON 13

25-30 MINUTES

1. **WARM-UP EXERCISE (TECHNIQUE EXERCISE, P.71) [5 MINUTES]**
   EX. 5b
   Practice the exercise 3 times

2. **D MINOR SCALE (1 OCTAVES) (P.74) [5 MINUTES]**
   a.   RIGHT HAND: Natural minor, start from D4 (3 times)
   b.   LEFT HAND: Natural minor, start from D3 (3 times)
   c.   RIGHT HAND: Harmonic minor, start from D4 (3 times)
   d.   LEFT HAND: Harmonic minor, start from D3 (3 times)

   > D minor and _____ major both use the same key signature!

3. **SONG: SCARBOROUGH FAIR (P.55-56) [15 MINUTES]**
   LEFT HAND
   a.   Practice this sequence below (5 times)

   > | Dm - - | Dm - - | C - - | Dm - - |

   b.   Practice the chord pattern in the song (5 times)

   > How many phrases are there in this song?
   > Now draw some phrase marks on the score!

   RIGHT HAND
   c.   Practice each phrase (5 times)

   HANDS TOGETHER
   d.   Practice each phrase (5 times)

   e.   *CHALLENGE*: Play the whole song smoothly 5 times!

4. THEORY TIME: MORE ON RHYTHM [8 MINUTES]
Write down some rhythmic patterns in 3/4 time and clap them out loud!

$\frac{3}{4}$ | | | ‖

$\frac{3}{4}$ | | | ‖

$\frac{3}{4}$ | | | ‖

5. SIGHT-READING (P.82) [5 MINUTES]
EX. 25 and 26
Check before you play!
1. Are they treble and bass clefs?

2. Look at the key signature

3. Look at the time signature

4. Find the first notes for both hands on the keyboard

5. Place your hands on the starting position

6. Count 2 bars before playing

7. You can start now

SCARBOROUGH FAIR

English Folk Song
Arr. Teresa Wong

SCARBOROUGH FAIR

OWN VERSION

PRACTICE RECORD

	Day 1	Day 2	Day 3	Day 4	Day 5	Day 6	Day 7
1							
2							
3							
4							
5							

STUDENT'S COMMENTS	TEACHER'S COMMENTS

LESSON 14

25-30 MINUTES

1. D MINOR ARPEGGIO: GOING UP AND DOWN (1 OCTAVE) (P.75) [5 MINUTES]
   a.   RIGHT HAND: Starting on D4 (5 times)
   b.   LEFT HAND: Starting on D3 (5 times)

2. SONG: MORE ON IMPROVISATION [15 MINUTES]
   a.   Practice this sequence below (3 times)

Dm	Dm	C	Dm
Dm	Dm	C	Dm
Dm	Dm	C	Dm
Dm	Dm	C	Dm

   b.   Use this sequence and compose a RIGHT HAND melody on top of it.
        Is the song in 3 times or in 4 times?

   c.   When you feel ready, try this sequence:

Dm	Dm	F	Dm
Dm	Dm	C	Dm
Dm	Dm	F	Dm
Dm	Dm	C	Dm

PRACTICE RECORD

	Day 1	Day 2	Day 3	Day 4	Day 5	Day 6	Day 7
1							
2							

STUDENT'S COMMENTS	TEACHER'S COMMENTS

LESSON 15

25-30 MINUTES

1. G MAJOR SCALE: GOING UP AND DOWN (2 OCTAVES) (P.74) [5 MINUTES]
   a.   RIGHT HAND: Starting from G4 (3 times)
   b.   LEFT HAND: Starting from G3 (3 times)
   c.   *CHALLENGE*: play hands together smoothly 3 times! (4 notes= 66)

2. G MAJOR ARPEGGIO: GOING UP AND DOWN (1 OCTAVE) (P.75) [5 MINUTES]
   a.   RIGHT HAND: Starting from G4 (3 times)
   b.   LEFT HAND: Starting from G3 (3 times)
   c.   *CHALLENGE*: play hands together smoothly 3 times! (2 notes= 66)

3. SONG: WHEN THE SAINTS GO MARCHING IN (P.64-65) [15 MINUTES]
RIGHT HAND
   a.   Sing the song in solfège
   b.   Practice bars 1-7 (5 times)
   c.   Practice bars 8-11 (5 times)
   d.   Practice bars 12-16 (5 times)
LEFT HAND
   e.   Practice bars 1-7 (5 times)
   f.   Practice bars 8-11 (5 times)
   g.   Practice bars 12-16 (5 times)
HANDS TOGETHER
   h.   Practice bars 1-7 (5 times)
   i.   Practice bars 8-11 (5 times)
   j.   Practice bars 12-16 (5 times)
   k.   *CHALLENGE*: Play the whole song smoothly 3 times!

4. THEORY TIME: MORE ON RHYTHM [8 MINUTES]
Write down some rhythmic patterns in 4/4 time and clap them out loud!

$\frac{4}{4}$ | | | ||

$\frac{4}{4}$ | | | ||

$\frac{4}{4}$ | | | ||

5. SIGHT READING (P.82) [5 MINUTES]
EX. 27 and 28
Check before you play!
1. Are they treble and bass clefs?
2. Look at the key signature
3. Look at the time signature
4. Find the first notes for both hands on the keyboard
5. Place your hands on the starting position
6. Count 2 bars before playing
7. You can start now

WHEN THE SAINTS GO MARCHING IN

American gospel hymn
Arr. Teresa Wong

WHEN THE SAINTS GO MARCHING IN

Piano 1 . 1

Piano 2 . 2

Piano 1 . 1

Piano 2 . 2

PRACTICE RECORD

	Day 1	Day 2	Day 3	Day 4	Day 5	Day 6	Day 7
1							
2							
3							
4							
5							

STUDENT'S COMMENTS	TEACHER'S COMMENTS

MANUSCRIPT PAPER

MANUSCRIPT PAPER

TECHNIQUE EXERCISE

ONE NOTE

Ex. 1b

Wrist To The Right Side

Wrist To The Left Side

TWO NOTES

Ex. 2a

Ex. 2b

THREE NOTES

Ex. 3a

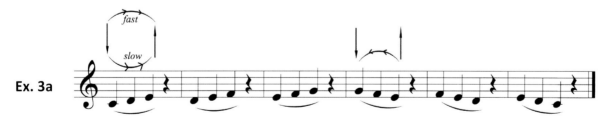

TECHNIQUE EXERCISE

FIVE NOTES

Ex. 4a

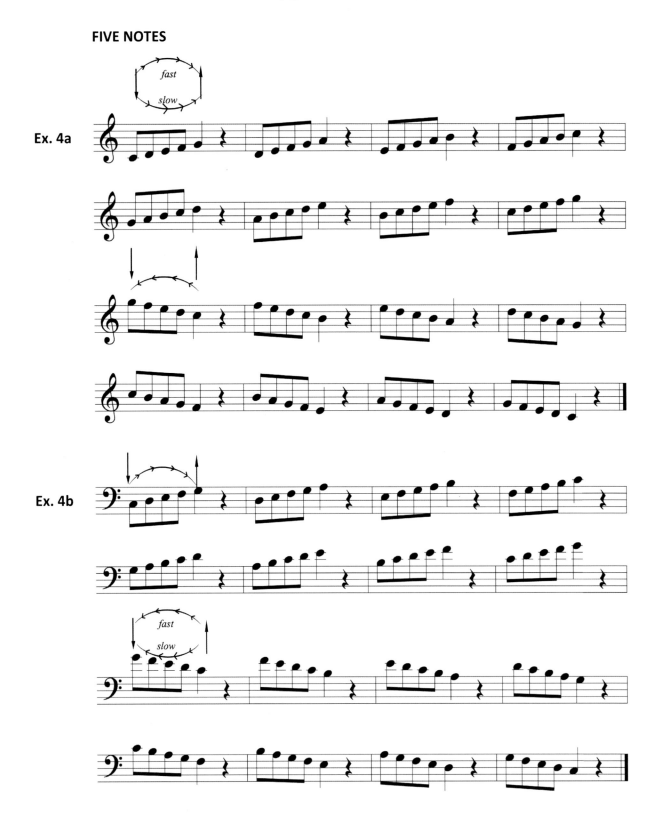

Ex. 4b

TECHNIQUE EXERCISE

FIVE-NOTE VARIATION

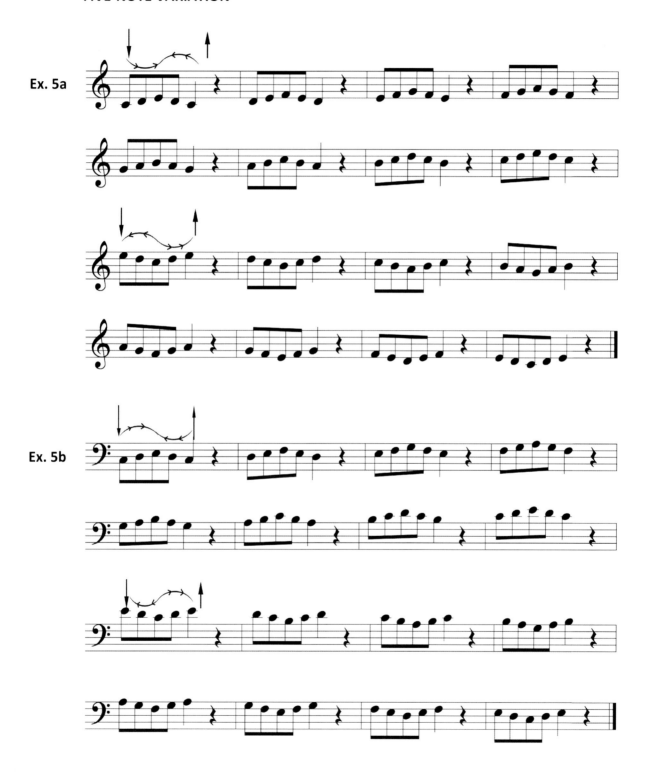

Ex. 5a

Ex. 5b

TECHNIQUE EXERCISE

EXERCISE IN 5THS

BROKEN CHORD

ONE-NOTE VARIATION

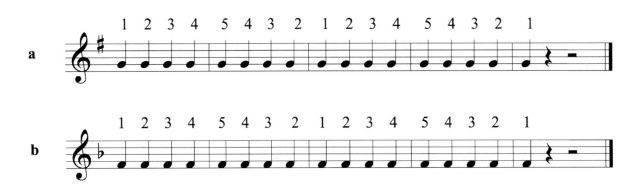

TECHNIQUE EXERCISE

TWO-NOTE VARIATION

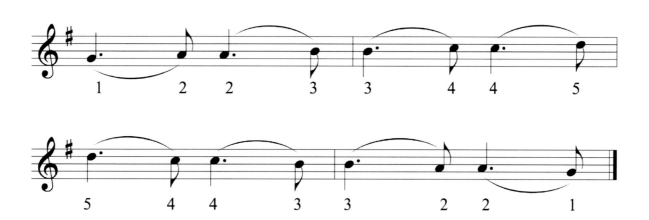

SCALES

G MAJOR: SIMILAR MOTION

F MAJOR: SIMILAR MOTION

D NATURAL MINOR: SIMILAR MOTION

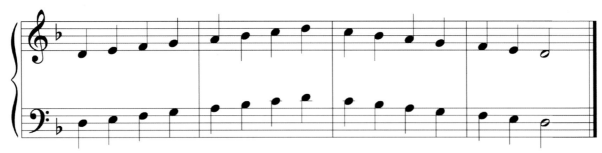

D HARMONIC MINOR: SIMILAR MOTION

ARPEGGIOS

G MAJOR: ARPEGGIO

F MAJOR: ARPEGGIO

D MINOR: ARPEGGIO

SIGHT READING

SIGHT READING

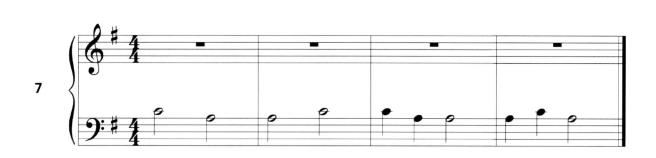

SIGHT READING

SIGHT READING

13

14

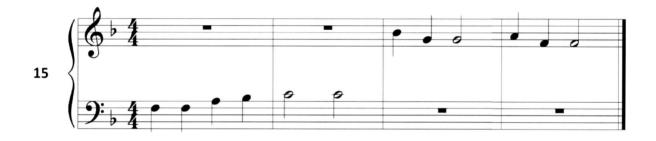

15

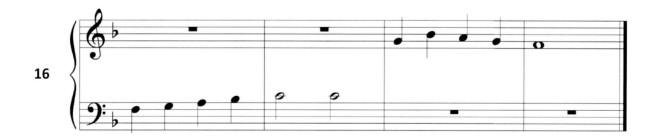

16

SIGHT READING

SIGHT READING

SIGHT READING

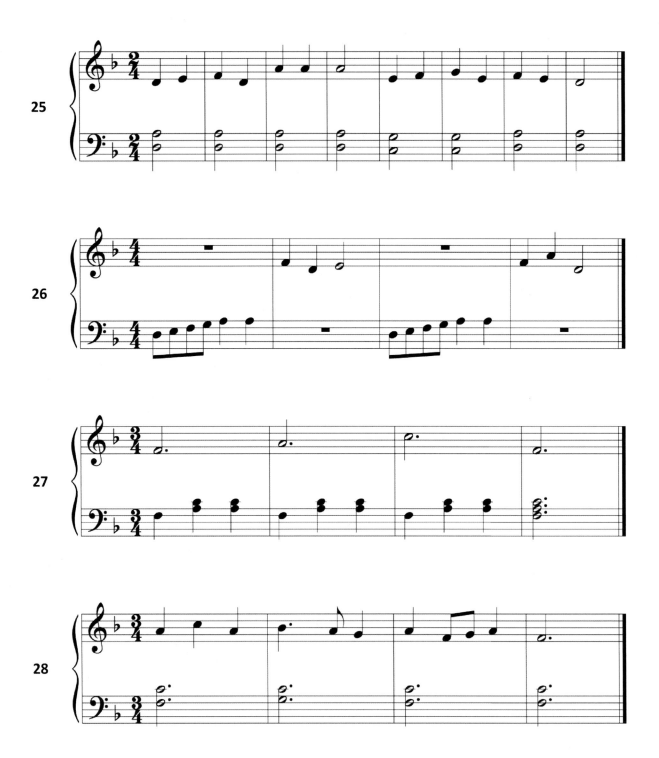

AURAL TRAINING

Let's do some warm up exercises. G Major this time!
*You can sing an octave lower if the pitches are too high for you

d   r   m   f   s   l   t   d'

Now try this!

d r d m d f   d s   d l   d t   d d'

Let's guess what your teacher's playing!

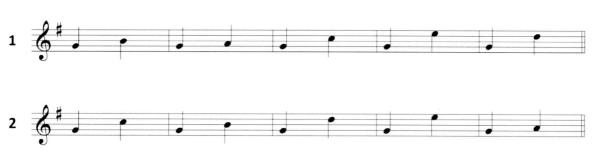

AURAL TRAINING

Level up! Let's sing three notes, here we go!

Let's check the answers!

(1) d m / d r / d f / d l / d s
(2) d f / d m / d s / d l / d r
(3) d r / d s / d l / d t / d d'
(4) d d' / d t / d s / d m / d r
(5) d m / d s / d f / d l / d r
(6) d r m / d m s / r f m / r m f / m r d
(7) d m f / f r s / m d f / d s d' / s m f
(8) d r m / d r l / d f l / d r f / d l d'
(9) d f m / d l s / d m r / d s f / d d' t
(10) d t l / d r l / d s r / d l f / d t f

AURAL TRAINING

Let's try it in F Major!
Can you sing the scale going up and going down?

d   r   m   f   s   l   t   d'   t   l   s   f   m   r   d

Now try this!

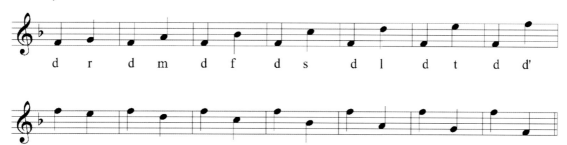

d   r   d   m   d   f   d   s   d   l   d   t   d   d'

d'   t   d'   l   d'   s   d'   f   d'   m   d'   r   d'   d

Let's sing three notes in F Major, here we go!

AURAL TRAINING

Level up! Let's sing four notes, here we go!

Let's try different rhythmic patterns!

Let's check the answers!

(11) d r m / s l d' / m l s / f r m / l s d'
(12) l s m / d' f l / l s t / r s m / d' t s
(13) d' s l / t l f / l m s / s m d / f d m
(14) t d' t / d' s l / t l s / m s r / f s l
(15) d m s d' / d f l d' / d' t l s / d' s f m / s m d d'
(16) m d s m / r d f s / m s l d' / l m s r / f l m d
(17) m f s d / r f s d / l s l f / d' s d' l / l d' t d'
(18) d s l m / d r d s / f s l m / r s m d / m s m f
(19) d m f s d / m r d r m / s f m d d / d' t l t d' / s l s f m
(20) m r m f s / l s f m r / d' d' t d' / d m s f s / f m r s d
(21) s l s m r d / d' t l s m r / m f m s d' / d d d r m / s f m r d

ABOUT THE AUTHOR

Teresa Wing-Yin Wong received her musical training at Hong Kong Baptist University, where she graduated with first class majoring in Piano Performance (B.A. Music), along with many scholastic awards. She was also awarded with the Licentiate of the Royal Schools of Music in Piano Performance in the same year. She further studied at Indiana University Jacobs School of Music with scholarships, later awarded with a Master degree of Music in Piano Performance, with special interests in Piano Pedagogy and Choral Conducting. She is honored to have studied with great teachers such as Grace Lau Lively-Stones, Shigeo Neriki, Edward Auer and Jean-Louis Hagenauer (piano), David Chung (harpsichord), Carmen Telléz (choral conducting), and Carlos Montané (voice). Miss Wong has participated in well-renowned music festivals, and she has performed frequently as a soloist and chamber musician in Europe, North America, and the Greater China. She was an accompanist for the Scuola Italia Program for Opera Singers in Italy and for various concert tours in the United States.

In her native city Hong Kong, Miss Wong was a freelance keyboard player for the Hong Kong PhiLeft handarmonic Orchestra, a piano accompanist for Hong Kong Bach Choir and Opera Hong Kong Company, as well as a conductor and a piano accompanist at Hong Kong Children's Choir and Shatin District Board Children's Choir among many other posts. She has performed as a soloist and a collaborative musician at various local public venues and concert halls, and has also recorded solo and chamber music programs for RTHK Radio Four. Her recent performance engagement includes several concert appearances in China and France.

Being a versatile pianist, Miss Wong has also actively involved in the world of music academia and competitions. She was an adjunct lecturer at Hong Kong Baptist University, and a teaching assistant at the Chinese University of Hong Kong when pursuing her research interest in historical musicology. She has served as a jury in prestigious international piano competitions.

Other than hands-on teaching, Miss Wong is passionate about helping students to succeed in various platforms apart from piano lessons. Miss Wong is the first person ever to develop successful iPhone applications - Aural Training Grade 5 (free and full versions) - to train music aural ability specifically for standardized exams presented by Associated Boards of Royal Schools of Music (ABRSM) and other music exam boards alike. Her past projects include her charity organization "Teresa Wong Music Academy' which organized concerts and workshops to educate and inspire music lovers, students and teachers in the community. Her recent projects include publishing her new books - Piano Freedom, Piano Technique Transformation Exercise Book, and Music on Wings: Piano Beginner Course Book Series (Student Practice Guides and Teacher Instruction Guides).

Miss Wong is currently the director and principal of Teresa Wong School of Music, which is her primary focus to train piano teachers and piano students to maintain a high level of teaching quality and learning standard. She is also the chief executive officer of Music on Wings Publications, and a member of the Music Teachers National Association (MNTA).

http://www.teresawong.hk/

Made in the USA
Coppell, TX
12 September 2023

21322933R00057